Waiting

For Margaret + Paul –
With my very best wishes

Ron

Also by Ronald Moran

Poetry (Books and Chapbooks)

The Blurring of Time
Diagramming the Clear Sky
Saying These Things
Greatest Hits, 1965-2000
Fish Out of Water
Getting the Body to Dance Again
Sudden Fictions
Life on the Rim
So Simply Means the Rain

Criticism

Four Poets and the Emotive Imagination (with co-author)
Louis Simpson

Waiting

Ronald Moran

CLEMSON UNIVERSITY
DIGITAL PRESS

Works produced at Clemson University by the Center for Electronic and Digital Publishing, including *The South Carolina Review* and its themed series "Virginia Woolf International," "Ireland in the Arts and Humanities," and "James Dickey Revisited," may be found at our Web site: http://www.clemson.edu/caah/cedp. Contact the director at 864-656-5399 for information.

CLEMSON UNIVERSITY
DIGITAL PRESS

Published by Clemson University Digital Press at the Center for Electronic and Digital Publishing, Clemson University, Clemson, South Carolina.

Produced with the Adobe Creative Suite CS4 and Microsoft Word. This book is set in Adobe Garamond Pro and was printed by Standard Register.

Editorial Assistant: Jordan McKenzie.

To order copies, contact the Center for Electronic and Digital Publishing, Strode Tower, Box 340522, Clemson University, Clemson, South Carolina 29634-0522. An order form is available at the digital press Web site (see above).

Table of Contents

ॐ

A Note on the Author

Acknowledgments

Some of the poems appeared originally in the following publications, sometimes in slightly different versions. I am grateful to the editors for permission to reprint them in this collection.

Abbey ("A Clearing Over Caesars Head," "Sitting at the End of a Long Row of Chairs"), *Iodine Poetry Review* ("English 101," "The Place," "Skeletons in the Closet") *The Louisiana Review* ("The Best Deer Tracker in Northern Louisiana"), *The Main Street Rag* ("Airing Out the Jacket," "Discoveries," "Heat Wave"), *Pudding Magazine* ("Playing Golf," "Waiting"), *The Revenant Culture* ("At the Lincoln Diner," "Lobsters"), *South Carolina Review* ("The Foo-Foo Girl," "Growing Up American," "Ice Storm," "July 4, 2007," "Marshlands," "Reading The Mail," "Silhouette in the Night Air," "Winds"), *Taproot Literary Review* ("Waking Up Tired"), *Tar River Poetry* ("South on the Interstate," Part 1 of 'Yard of the Month' of the three part poem of that name). "The Warranty" appeared in *The Pudding House Gang.* Columbus: Pudding House, 2009.

ৎ

Dedication

For Jennifer Bosveld, Wayne Chapman, and John Judson

Each of whom has been instrumental in helping me to be a poet, as well as in significantly advancing the cause of poetry through writing and/or editing and publishing.

Introduction

In one of his poems in this collection, Ronald Moran invites his reader to accompany him as he "enter[s] a room." It may be, the poem says, "smaller or larger than this one." In the room he may find "a new T-shirt to wear or to open a metal box / of my secrets." He adds, "I am not dreaming, though I might as well be." This verbal motion and flow, physical and mental, can enable him "to feel / better about my surroundings" and "remember why I walked down one short hallway to another" over the course of a lifetime. These phrases and lines from "Passages" disclose more about the poet and his poems than one might at first suspect.

The word "stanza," for example, in its Latin origins derives from a word meaning "room." The poet's invitation into the room is his invitation into the poem itself. Inside one is likely to find the quotidian things of a life governed by routine and ordinary things like T-shirts, but one may find a metal box that will reveal secrets, something under the cover of memory released and imposing its shape into the poem itself. Though the world he occupies is of the waking world, it "might as well" be called something like a dream.

In this remarkable new collection, Moran's tenth volume, one is aware of how this poet has crafted a style and voice uniquely his own, though the voice occasionally reminds one of other poets. Its development can be traced back to his first volume, *So Simply Means the Rain*, published more than forty years ago, and all the volumes that have followed. Before commenting on the content of these poems, I want to say something about the style itself.

Even when poems do not seem especially dream-like—and many do not—they possess an ever-expanding accretion of detail laid out in a syntax that is always nudging and pushing ahead toward a conclusion of both inevitability and surprise. There is great resilience and fluidity in such an unfettered style. Typically about 30-40 lines in length, the poems may consist of only one or two sentences. But these stretched-out units are notably uncluttered in their paratactic and hypotactic unfolding, in large part because of a pattern wherein a line of five or six stresses is immediately broken by a following line of only two stresses. Often the poems pivot on the succinct injections of those shortened lines. The poem builds upon these alternating couplets, themselves portioned out as, typically, about four couplets to a stanza. All the poems are busy, even crowded, but they appear to the eye and ear of the reader as supple and unconstrained.

The poems in this volume, *Waiting*, can be roughly categorized in two groups: those of a suburban, middle-class life of a South Carolinian acutely aware of the world outside his window, across the street, down the road, or perhaps a short drive into town. It is an ordinary world that craves the extraordinary, a mundane world often transformed into the amazing. A second category of poems involves a poet deeply centered in family life, one now embracing five generations and including a wife, Jane, plagued by a life-threatening illness.

Sometimes the world outside Moran's window appears hemmed in by the "rules" of a society overly-civilized. In "The Best Deer Tracker in Northern Louisiana," he brings together the woman who stands ahead of him at the meat section of the local supermarket, planning her dinner for sixteen dinner guests, and the poet's memories of a deer tracker, Lowell, a primitive force in his own right, famed for catching giant catfish and pulling them out of the water with his bloody fingers. We learn that all his teeth were pulled in a single day. The poem ends:

> . . . she watched her Tilapia or Sahimi Tuna turning into
> a giant cat,
>
> as blood dripped down Lowell's arm and him flashing
> his new smile
> to her and her 16 guests, and maybe her husband
> if she had one;
> and as the giant cat took shape, its spine slashing about,
> its whiskers red,
> her leaving the table, without excusing herself, and not
> returning.

In the hilarious and yet poignant "Yard of the Month," the poet is "waiting in my den for something big / to happen." Suddenly a sign indicating "Yard of the Month" is mistakenly staked into the front lawn. No gardening guru, he recalls naively watering plastic flowers installed by a neighbor until corrected by his daughter. The public designation, it seems, cannot be undone, and it inwardly calls him to task for want of commendatory credentials: "*No, Mom and Dad, / not exactly for my writing or for my teaching, and, uh, / as for my / public service, I've been pretty busy since I retired.*" A nosy and carping neighbor, the "woman in green," feeding his unworthiness, ridicules the award up and down the neighborhood. The poem ends as "guilt, that mythy // guardian, took hold of my head like a vice."

Enclosure in one's daily life, a life that appears to have selected the poet rather than the reverse, nonetheless churns up a variety of associations and regrets (like the "mythy guardian" at the end of "Yard of the Month")—from "the earlier nights / in Baghdad" in the Gulf War evoked by neighborhood fireworks in "July 4, 2007," to the hired PAL, a personal apologizer, who can "make the offended one feel good about hearing, / *Yes, indeed, my client was at fault* / —whatever the circumstances" in "The Art of Being Sorry," to the anniversary of the Nazi *Kristallnacht* that conjures this conclusion in "November 9":

> but we measure life by incidents, as in friends
> at the gate
>
> waiting for news, any news, who only want
> to be flying
> somewhere, anywhere, on a mission of light,
> to spread
>
> good news like mustard seeds over a land
> that is
> hardening before us like putty, like concrete
> newly poured.

The smallest and most unlikely episodes miraculously transform Moran's conventional world, making these poems constantly hail the unexpected and surprising: a thief hilariously smuggling lobsters in his pants ("Lobsters"), the 1450cc's of a big motorcycle that suddenly appears on his street ("Silhouette in the Night Air"), a Baltimore child-murderer ("Revolutions of the Moon"), or advertising brochures in "Reading the Mail."

Not since Donald Hall's poems about the fatal illness of his wife Jane Kenyon has a poet so delicately evoked the illness of his wife, another Jane, in this collection. Though the death of the poet's wife in 2009 had not yet occurred in these poems, it is wrenchingly anticipated. With "sedated sleep" relieving her of "a corridor of pain," the poem called "A Blessing" shows the poet clinging to his wife's receding presence: "So I cup her hand leisurely in mine, closing / it slowly, feeling her tremors until my hand / calms her, and I whisper, *Time to sleep.*" Over the course of his long career, Ronald Moran's poems celebrating his wife—what one might call the "Jane poems"—should now be assembled in a separate publication to trace his always steadying ties of love that span more than a half century without a trace of sentimentality or a single false note.

This poet continues to be haunted by the presence of both his deceased parents who return in memory and dream, not always soothingly, but in quest of some ultimate accommodation. Even their parents, his grandparents, impose their more distant calibrations. Children, grandchildren and a son-in-law drop in and out of the poems.

The power of the imagination can transform a world that is part-bewildering and part-prosaic, but for Ronald Moran always in the style of an inviting and companionable neighbor, like the man just down the street no better and no worse than yourself. Like the poems, the world is full of tricks and deviations and may seem at times almost but never quite overwhelming. In the end, the absurd world is fit only to be laughed at. What gives this poet life is his fixed place within it especially as he reckons his sustaining and multi-generational family ties. In a sense, place is all: "Only here will you survive," he exclaims in "The Place," "after light blisters / the landscape, / and the earth trembles to an anthem not / of its making." Such a place flees, as it does for all of us, but for this poet it does not fade.

George S. Lensing
Mann Family Distinguished Professor of English and Comparative Literature
University of North Carolina at Chapel Hill

Part One

The Best Deer Tracker in Northern Louisiana

I took a number, 53, in the meat section of the Fresh Market,
            to wait my turn
to buy eight large shrimp for Jane and me to dip in a spicy sauce,
            a small thing
but big on pleasure for us, as number 52, a thin, well-dressed,
            twitchy woman,
was being waited on at the fish case, pondering this,
            then that,

while the butcher was patiently counting his fingers
            for good luck,
since number 52 could not decide between Tilapia
            or Sashimi Tuna,
or how to prepare each, asking the butcher, who was
            not a gourmet chef,
how he would prepare the dish for her 16 guests
            for dinner tomorrow.

O how he wished he had a gourmet recipe book in back
            so he could say,
Excuse me M'am, I think I have just the dish for you
            and your guests;
while in between her questions and the intimacy
            with which she rattled off
her own recipes of Sockeye Salmon and Orange Roughy,
            the butcher

began fingering the blade of his fish knife, as if he were
            priming it,
when I thought of a friend of over 40 years ago, Lowell,
            the best
deer tracker in northern Louisiana, who used to fish
            for giant cats
with his fingers, under stumps, and raise them up with
            bloody fingers,

not feeling any pain then or ever, and who replaced
            all uppers and lowers
with false teeth in one day, and then I imagined him
            as one of her guests
tomorrow night, all seated at the table, and Lowell telling
            them his stories
as she watched her Tilapia or Sahimi Tuna turning into
            a giant cat,

as blood dripped down Lowell's arm and him flashing
                    his new smile
to her and her 16 guests, and maybe her husband,
                    if she had one;
and as the giant cat took shape, its spine slashing about,
                    its whiskers red,
her leaving the table, without excusing herself, and not
                    returning.

Airing Out The Jacket

After a night at the strip bar
I aired out my light, blue and white jacket out back
on the bare limb of a maple on a bright December day.

Maybe the dog next door caught the scent of the bar—
cigarette smoke, perfume, the damp and gritty underside
of the Bible Belt—and wanted some action,

or maybe it went into a barking frenzy because the jacket
was a threat, that it might, at any moment, flap its arms,
fly over the fence between us, assault him

on the deck he was guarding. Later, he stalked
the solid, board fence, growling, waiting for that moment
we wait for nervously, bravely, that could happen any time.

What else could I do but hang the jacket
on my lone tree left, a Bradford Pear, in front,
close to the street? Within an hour, a Board member

took its picture from her car's open window, murmuring
something about Article XII of the Homeowner's Covenant,
then said, louder, as she drove off, "That's one hell of an ornament."

Silhouette in the Night Air

If the bell rings do I have to answer the door,
                    and if I do
will this one be my last visitor? Not now.
                    Then
I hear a motorcycle, a big one, coming down
                    my street
revving up its 1450cc's to a level that outdoes
                    the lowest DC-9's

on our landing pattern, to which all of us have
                    adjusted,
but not to the muffler, or lack thereof, of a bike
                    shifting gears
in front of my house, while I think, with some envy,
                    I suppose,
Why I can't be out there stirring up the air,
                    letting

the Home Owners' Association know that, yes,
                    Here I am!
You just try to root me out in your newsletter
                    and, yeah,
maybe this is the bike I want to be on at this time
                    in my life—
late going—not that much ahead, and I think I know
                    this story,

but I want to be out there, too, and why not?
                    Why not
try to split apart the night air with my silhouette
                    of heat?
No roadside bombs, but dark shoulders and curves
                    that beckon
like a siren, *Come closer. Try me out. I'm waiting
                    just for you.*

YARD OF THE MONTH

I Yard of the Month

Once more I'm waiting in my den for something big
              to happen,
when I hear my mailbox being slammed shut
              and see a red car
making a quick turnaround in the driveway across
              the street,

so I go outside to see if I need to call the bomb squad
              or just
toss away another drive-by advertisement for cleaning
              my gutters,
when, whoa, there's a sign in front of my boxwoods,
              "Yard of the Month."

My yard? With a chartreuse hose stretched out like a snake
              on warm rocks
on the south side, where I should, at the least, have planted
              some weeds,
and on the other side, my Oneal Sanitation trash barrel
              in full view

from the street, in direct contradiction of the Covenant;
              and now a dead
Bradford Pear in front due to be cut down and removed
              later today,
the only dead tree I know of in my neighborhood,
              beside those

in the waste zone in back, where not even a tree service
              will go
without shots, as if they were entering the Congo Basin,
              and then,
I open my mailbox and there it is, the congratulatory
              notice of my winning,

but the name's wrong, and it belongs down the street
              to 332 not 322;
and after I do what I should to correct the clerical error,
              the next morning

the red car appears, quickly disappears, and the sign's back
          and now I know

what this day will be like, and after I try to fix the compass
          of my world,
I receive an email from the president of the Association
          saying, yes, indeed,
your yard won, with *CONGRATULATIONS* in large caps,
          and I want to tell

someone, but Jane is sleeping off her pain, so I call my
          dead parents
to tell them of their only son's finally having won something.
          No, Mom and Dad,
not exactly for my writing or for my teaching, and, uh,
          as for my

public service, I've been pretty busy since I retired. Oh
          the award,
it's a special horticultural thing, given on the basis of
          committee decision.
Money, not really, but wait, my other phone is ringing.
          I'll call you back.

    II Flowers

I am looking through thin openings of a blind
          slatting
my wide palladium window facing the street,
          when I see
the woman in green who haunts the sidewalks
          mornings, afternoons,
and, after returning home, waits for some child
          to enter her yard

so that she can call the sheriff, or at the least,
          tell the child
to leave, and resume her waiting until time comes
          to walk her mile
route again, making mental notes to tell our
          neighbors
how to dress up their properties, the woman
          who cried out

to a neighbor when I won "Yard of the Month"
               by pure accident—
a classic case of mistaken identity that I tried
               unsuccessfully
to correct—*I see we are now giving awards*
               for plastic flowers,
to which he replied, *You don't know how hard*
               Ron tried

to refuse that "Yard of the Month" award; and
               yes, it is true
I had no idea that the flowers my kind neighbor
               planted below
my mailbox were plastic, a cure to the case
               of slow death
to everything else anyone tried to plant there
               before.

I even watered the flowers during the drought,
               by hand
and by sprinkler, and I suppose my neighbors
               who saw me
were not surprised, not because they thought
               the flowers
were real, but because, well, I'm the one who,
               after drinking

three wines, slipped off the stairs to my garage
               while taking out
the trash, and an ironing board fell on top of me,
               covering me
like a slab, and, as I called out to Jane, neighbors
               across the street
heard and came to my rescue, and word spread
               like a cold in school.

Three nights ago, my daughter, Sally, whose house
               backs up
to the woman in green, said, before going home,
               You know
She's right. Those flowers are not real, which is
               OK with me,
but now I will only water them before the drought
               strikes.

III The Woman in Green

I was standing in my short, squatty driveway,
        trying
to absorb a few minutes of Vitamin D from
        a dying sun,
when here comes the woman in green
        taking

one of her two daily walks, probably noting
        whose trash cans
are visible from the street, whose lawns are
        climbing
with weeds, and whose bushes look like ghetto
        rejects,

the woman who knew months before I did
        that my flowers
in front were plastic and spread the word around
        the neighborhood.
I think everyone has a woman in green close by,
        one who has

to do or say only a few things for us to single
        her out—
as in, *Keep your children out of my yard*, or telling
        a neighbor
of *A tree that should really be cut down very soon*,
        but then—

maybe, and, well, perhaps this is only a *maybe*,
        but suppose
she is in her mid-sixties and so far has led a life
        inconsolable
with compassion, understanding, the virtues
        we associate,

with people, well, that we like, whose failings,
        if any,
we overlook like a worn jacket in a closet—
        but, anyway,
I said something flippant to her about telling
        my neighbors

about my flowers and bemoaning the fact
                              of my award
for "Yard of the Month," howsoever ill-deserved
                              the award was,
and, oh yes, I tried to give it back and pass it on.
                              No luck.

When twilight paid a brief visit, I thought,
                              Why?
Why should I even care what she says or does,
                              which I don't,
I kept trying to convince myself, but guilt,
                              that mythy

guardian, took hold of my head like a vice,
                              trying to tell me
of something I did not understand and probably
                              never will,
but, hey, I tried and if I failed, I failed the only way
                              I knew how.

Pennies

For no reason I think of Parks Diner in Waterville
            and of the waitress
who told my three friends and me, told us—
            not asked us—

to empty our pockets and give her all our pennies
            for a tip,
before we were even served our burgers and fries.
            Soundlessly

we complied, and while I do not know how much
            of our loot
she gathered in her apron, I know she is gone,
            like Parks Diner;

and I think of how our government will soon issue
            new pennies
and I wonder, At what cost and of what materials,
            seriously,

since the penny, like a diner, is out of fashion.
            No grandfathers
like mine dig their fingers into their purses for coins,
            including pennies.

I have been waiting for their obituary for years,
            but the government
wants to keep Abe Lincoln front and center at least
            somewhere.

Will they be made out of copper, the contractors'
            nightmare—
now that copper is worth more than the chance
            of getting caught,

as arrest citations report daily in local papers?
            And now
I am reeling back to World War II, or whatever
            it is called now,

when in 1943, pennies were steel coated with zinc,
                    while copper
was used for shell casings, and I thought then, Wow,
                    what super coins!

but I never saved any for my future, whatever that is
                    to a seven year old.
So pennies are back in, in my seventies, and what
                    will the people do?

Act as I did, the innocent, or hoard them in boxes
                    in Saran Wrap,
for the duration, howsoever long that may be,
                    in a secure drawer.

WINDS

APRIL 2007

While I watch Lou Dobbs' grisly accounting each night
                    of casualties,
I also hear Ralph Bristol's argument on talk radio
                    that the Iraq War

is our cheapest war, our dead the lowest of all wars,
                    and I hear his jaw
clenching and see his face burning at the liberal callers
                    he says don't care

about facts, as if these are the only costs, as the winds
                    sweep over
the mid-Atlantic states, driving water over sandbags,
                    tossing trailers

like the fragile limbs of a Bradford Pear, when I think
                    of William Stafford:
a pacifist, conscientious objector during World War II,
                    the poet

who wrote the most about winds, maybe because
                    of his childhood
in Hutchinson, Kansas, all wind, sky, and level horizons,
                    and who wrote,

"This is the field where the battle did not happen,"
                    from his long-titled
"At the Un-National Monument Along the Canadian Border,"
                    which Gilbert Allen

read last Friday night at Leopard Forest Café in Travelers Rest,
                    and as he read,
the winds started climbing the Southern Appalachians,
                    gathering force

like a late summer storm in the Caribbean, cruise ships
                    changing course
like a troop carrier in the sandstorm of a war
                    no one wins.

JULY 4, 2007

It feels like a Saturday, coming as it does
               on a Wednesday,
and except for no mail, no banks, and some
               store closings,

it is a nondescript Saturday, my neighbors
               cutting grass,
painting, or planting, but by 5:00 p.m. supplies
               of hot dogs,

ground beef, and buns will have disappeared
               from supermarkets;
and by 9:00 p.m. our town in South Carolina,
               the fireworks center

of America, will sound like the earlier nights
               in Baghdad,
while a CNN or Fox newscaster is trying not
               to cringe

in front of the camera, as America wipes out
               the powers of evil
in the Mideast, and the rest of us are stunned
               by the bravery

of newscasters in bombings depicted for us
               so closely,
just as, for a little while, the men and women
               of northern Virginia—

safe from harm, dressed in Sunday finery as if
               for a cotillion—
watched, instead, the battle of First Manassas,
               June 21, 1861,

first hand through opera glasses, until the fat lady
               never sang,
and war for us as a spectator sport was changed
               forever.

DISCOVERIES

They are finding turtles and infinitesimal
                    creatures
thought to be extinct or to have never
                    existed,
in the swamps of Vietnam, South America,
                    and Africa,
or in the electron microscopes of hush-hush
                    laboratories,

moving with impunity through a world
                    that gave up
on finding them again or ever finding them;
                    and now
textbooks are being revised every six months,
                    new editions
popping out like hives on researchers,
                    who can

barely contain their excitement, while AM
                    talk show hosts
descry the discoveries as another sad instance
                    of liberals
trying to discount the biblical story of creation.
                    Meanwhile
 the green sections of supermarkets grow
                    into aisles

and the people are asking, some for the first time,
                    Where were we?
and I want to know, too, and I still cannot shake
                    the image
of a squid the size of a submarine or of soldiers
                    riding in Humvees
soft on armor, toward roadside bombs soon to be
                    unearthed.

Heat Wave

It was a prickly day. Holly shrubs poked
                    outward
with their winsome spines, not aimed
                    maliciously,

I think, but out of boredom at the lack
                    of relief
from a heat wave that hung on too long
                    for June—

the temperature nudging 100 degrees
                    three days
in a row—so that the mosquitoes, sluggish,
                    short on water,

hung around doorways and windows, looking
                    for an opening
into the wet—blood or no blood—taking
                    whatever

moisture presented itself; and as soon as
                    we began
to complain about carrying out the trash
                    to the street,

I realized, O good Jesus, what kind of a life
                    am I leading
if that's a problem, and when these moments
                    of self doubt

lower me a notch on my self-esteem ladder,
                    I think
of toting backpacks, a belt full of equipment,
                    and a M-16,

the sun indifferent and sand, its ally, randomly
                    tossing
its knives, cutting at will, the air cloudy, thick,
                    compliant.

The Place

for C. M.

There is a place where there is no wind.
                    Smoke
rises vertically until it is motionless;
                    the scent
of gardenia does not play on the senses,
                    but rises
until the air pales and thins, where voices
                    die out,
and music—one antidote to the sadness
                    abounding—
caught in flight amid whole and half notes.
                    And you ask,
Why is it here? to which the place answers,
                    Because
only here will you survive after light blisters
                    the landscape
and the earth trembles to an anthem not
                    of its making.

WAITING

I ask myself, How do I feel being in my 70's?
                    Pretty good,
I suppose, just to be here, for the moment
                    at least,
which may change momentarily, but if I try
                    to look
too far ahead, I could be as still as a mailbox,
                    so for now

I have nothing else to say, unless I invent
                    an option
used daily by officials in charge of the health
                    and welfare
of nations—a mouthful, I know, but, hey,
                    true as a compass,
none of which having anything to do with me
                    waiting

for something to happen or not to happen,
                    when,
a jet skims my rooftop, and I doubt it will
                    ever make it
to the end of the runway but I only hear a Civic
                    out front,
modified, low to the road, burning the asphalt,
                    leaving a trail

of fire like a smart missile locked in horizontally,
                    and I'm certain
it will never navigate the curve up the street.
                    Wrong, again.
So I'm thinking, Is this how it's going to be:
                    reality
a blush in the sky that declares the next day,
                    a trip

to the bathroom at 6:00 am, then back to bed,
                    to dream
in some alternate psyche of a Whirl-a-Twirl,
                    a Scream-an-Eagle,
or a roller coaster on its last run, just as its cars
                    lean hard
into a high curve, and everyone is screaming
                    as if alive.

LOBSTERS

While most of us on the east coast doubted
                                how anyone
could smuggle six live lobsters in his pants
                                without
howling, as his pants exuded both salt water
                                and, well,
even saltier water, when we, the innocents,
                                did not know

that lobsters in San Diego have no pincers,
                                and whatever
does this mean other than we did not know,
                                when a native,
 of Torresdale, a suburb of Philadelphia, said
                                O come now!
Everyone knows lobsters there are harmless.
                                So we add

this bit of info to our network, slowing down
                                as the days
yawn before nightfall but still awake enough
                                to pick up
what we can and lodge it wherever our neurons
                                on a good day
let us, linking one with the other and showing us,
                                if not Mensa types—

at least aware and alert as we were meant to be—
                                and, hey,
they're going to nail this guy for robbing the pots
                                again
and it will stick, the lobsters still alive, scuttling
                                across the bottom,
defenseless, but under guard, waiting to be called
                                to testify.

A Rising

Bodiless, like wisps of smoke on windless days,
they rose beyond the limits of smoke, as if
balloons were freed from the deck of a party,
helium filled on another windless day, but wind
is never absent, only perceived to be, as when
a hand is brushing back loose, stray hairs.

Not the holy spirit or the granules of the past,
but strands of memory freed up of their own will,
and visible but once to us, when our secrets
and our longings reach a commingling peace,
like an accord, but not as if they were at war,
or, say, like the part of a pear hidden in a still life,

always there, supporting the whole, as in what
rose that day, formless, but once filled with life.

Part Two

THE FOO-FOO GIRL

The foo-foo girl did a bad thing and went
                    to jail,
and Mommy and Daddy couldn't stop
                    their little
foo-foo girl from going to jail but they
                    could

have the jail moved into their foo-foo
                    girl's house,
which they did with the aid of Barbie
                    and Ken,
who is now an FBI agent in charge of
                    monitoring

the whereabouts of bad foo-foo girls,
                    at least
foo-foo girls who did bad things such as,
                    well,
we all know because the media also loves
                    foo-foo girls

with oh so fine long hair with pure roots
                    and midriffs
sculpted into midriffs, even with tattoos
                    of spiders,
and those long, sinuous legs, the thighs
                    of which,

according to the *Foo-Foo Girls Handbook,*
                    lengthen
into inscrutability. Our foo-foo girl had to wear
                    a bracelet
that Ken clasped ever so gently around
                    her ankle,

after having gone with Barbie to Tiffany's
                    to pick out
one approved by the *Handbook* on page 37,
                    after which
the foo-foo girl said, *Party!* and her house—
                    the jail—

was magically filled with other foo-foo girls
                    and escorts,
champagne, tinkling glasses, music, mood lifters
                    in bathrooms,
and then all the loopy, pretty people said,
                    Foo-foo!

THE WARRANTY

The only call I received on my 72nd birthday
          began,
We have a wonderful surprise for you, Ronald,
          which

roused me from my lethargy to ask: What if
          The New Yorker
wrongly sent me a rejection notice for a poem
          I sent?

Or some foundation or society had given me
          an award
for lifetime achievement—for what?—but hope,
          like a virus,

still hung on, so I replied to the tinkling voice,
          Please tell me,
by which time my spirits were dancing like the limbs
          of a Bradford Pear,

when the voice said, still tinkling, but pitched higher,
          A great deal
on a five-year extended warranty on your car!
          to which

I replied, *I'm 72 and if you guarantee that I'll live*
          to my late 70's
we have a deal. Silence, except for a background
          of *Say what?*

When the voice finally returned, it said, soberly,
          I'm sorry, sir,
but I can only extent the warranty on your car,
          not your life.

SKELETONS IN THE CLOSET

I overheard the skeletons in my closet talking
                    of the difference
between the living and the dead, and agreeing,
                    unanimously,

that, once the piranhas of time finished feasting
                    on their bodies,
only the flesh made any difference, and then
                    I spoke up—

the interloper—You must mean the temptations
                    of the flesh,
to which they replied, without pause, On them
                    we thrive:

gluttonies, carnal desires, lists in your holy books,
                    without which
 we would be homeless. We mean the flesh, the sac
                    holding

your organs in place that you hang on us like barbells,
                    expecting us
to keep fit, to accommodate your weighty demands
                    like athletes,

so we must suffer like beasts in jungles, in basins,
                    or in
the dry, dreary plains, and endure your poundings
                    on asphalt,

as well as the hammerings of your contact sports,
                    the metaphor
of daily concourse, your trafficking in winning, which,
                    without doubt,

you never achieve, or else we would not be here
                    to testify—
our slight posturing, invisible, except to the touch
                    of bony truth.

Tearing

The eyes of my friend James, which is not his name,
                    began tearing up
without any known cause after he retired,
                    except that
they said he had a *sensitivity*—a medical word
                    with no history—

to something no one, especially James, could
                    figure out,
and which occurred at inopportune times,
                    such as,
when representing his church as a lay member
                    to a convention

of some importance, where the keynote address
                    was given
by a cleric with a name heard around the world,
                    James teared up—
not cried, there being a huge difference between
                    the two—

while thanking the speaker, and as they rolled
                    down his cheeks,
one fell on a paper of his holiness. At Toys 'R Us,
                    while looking
for a gift for his grandchild, his tearing took over,
                    bringing

to his side two clerks who asked him, *What's wrong?*
                    to which
he replied, *I can't find my toy,* which, well, confounded
                    the clerks
since the response to James's problem did not exist
                    in their manual,

but Channel 5 was in the store interviewing the manager
                     and filming
the newly emptied shelves of toys made in China,
                    when the crew
heard the clerks in distress and filmed James
                    in the midst

of a downpour, ran it on the 6:00 Evening News,
                    where it was
picked up by a major network, making James
                    instantly
famous, a talk show circuit rider, and a latter day
                    Jeremiah.

THE ART OF BEING SORRY

Today I do not want to read *No New Messages,*
                    so I am sending
myself an email about the newest in a line
                    of occupations
designed to lower our stress levels, to lead us
                    to the good life,
as Drs. Phil, Laura and other miracle workers
                    would have us;

and I am thinking of a man and woman who sat
                    across the aisle
from me in a train from New York to New Haven,
                    and who said
to each other, *I am sorry;* and as they got off
                    at Stamford,
I think they were still angry, upset, tense,
                    and miserable.

Not so, if they could have hired the services
                    of a PAL,
a Personal Apologizer, not to be confused
                    with a PA,
a Personal Assistant whose duties may include,
                    on rare occasions,
an apology for a client but rarely rendered
                    like a pro,

as one is trained to do at community colleges
                    offering curricula
in PAL, not leading you to a diploma to hang
                    in an office,
but, rather, to a small certificate, plastic coated
                    for pocket or purse,
like the ID of a plainclothes cop or an FBI agent.
                    The PAL

is schooled in feeling the client's humiliation, shame,
                frantic need
to admit being wrong—dead wrong—or responsible
                and hence
is able to make the offended one feel good about
                hearing,
Yes, indeed, my client was at fault—whatever
                the circumstances

and whoever: family, business associate, friend
                nurse, neighbor,
or, for example, the SUV driver your client cut off
                at an intersection
who flashed the bird, but your client got his license
                for you,
and, of course, you must also be skilled at securing
                information

not usually available to the rest of us; and finally,
                the PAL
should be a middle child or maybe an only child,
                since from birth
one was taught to feel inferior, the other guilty,
                and whatever
each one did for the first 18 years was incorrect
                to someone.

KING DAVID STYLE CENTER

As I was trying to leave King David Style Center
    before the rain
slid down Paris Mountain, Jane was saying
    long goodbyes

to Danny, Betty, Cathy, and Pam, with me
    adding
small urgings, as in *Looks like, rain, Jane.*
    Let's go,

or making the smallest of talk with the staff
    when a woman
waiting for us to reverse the magnetic poles
    of King David's,

said to me, *You're from Philadelphia. Right?*
    What?
I recoiled, as if I'd hit the wall in a marathon,
    and replied,

Born in Philadelphia and lived there until 1946.
    How'd you know?
She came back with, *My ex-laws live there,*
    and I said,

You're the only person to ever say that to me,
    to which
she answered, *It's not really much of an accent,*
    but it's there.

In the car, heading back home in upstate SC,
    I thought
of Archille Biron's *Ah oui! La magnifique oreille*
    d'un linguiste appliqué.

NOVEMBER 9

On this day, the Nazis ignited the *Kristallnacht,*
                    while earlier,
by a generation, Kaiser Wilhelm II announced
                    his abdication

of the throne, then lit out for the Netherlands,
                    all, of course,
so long ago no one remembers but students
                    of history—

as it always is, unless an event stirs up
                    the media,
who fire broadsides before the event even
                    opens its arms.

Meanwhile, as newsworthy as a softball game,
                    UAL
cancelled another flight, this one, though,
                    with my friends

booked on it, which qualifies for us, at our age,
                    as an incident.
And, hey, what is happening to our country?
                    I know nothing

will ever equal the Holocaust or pogroms
                    in the Congo;
but we measure life by incidents, as in friends
                    at the gate

waiting for news, any news, who only want
                    to be flying
somewhere, anywhere, on a mission of light,
                    to spread

good times like mustard seeds over a land
                    that is
hardening before us like putty, like concrete
                    newly poured.

Revolutions of the Moon

And if the revolutions of the moon do not account
for the madness off the streets, as with the guy
in Baltimore who killed his three kids, then
cut himself, here and there, to make it look real,

and if not Baltimore, it is Detroit or Houston
or Charlotte or a suburb of Chicago, with pillars
in front, a concrete pool, and, sure, two bodies,
and what I am asking is, Was it always this way

and we never knew, or is it a modern trend, like
a high end movie or computer game or new study
by a PhD in health from the West Coast or from
the East Coast, or, for that matter, any coast,

as long as we all know about it and can safely add it
to our box labeled *Culture*? And now I am thinking,
Am I like them and, if so, what's the cure? What
pills, money, change in milieu, new relationship?

One doctor cups his chin, another runs her hands
through her hair, which loops down the silky trail
of her spine, and I know I am drifting, but so,
What do we do, what can we do, and should I try?

MARSHLANDS

If the antidote is less potent than the disease
and, finally, after single doses of well-being,
we start failing but miraculously recover, what
reasons are there: divine intervention, the quick
and slick moves of the government, that fear
is only fear, with a substance no more than that
of a summer moth fluttering its life away before

the patio lights on your property, not mine where
the back waste zone is a danger even to the TV
crews of reality shows. Which one does not matter,
since each of us is living one every day, and why
complicate our lives for pay or press or whatever
the reward for being instantly recognized as one
who will eat worms on demand, while here and there,

in the marshlands of Savannah, the sleek Osprey
feed on bright, silver fish that feed on minnows, as
the old guys, out every day, catch baby hammerheads
and long, skinny ladyfish that may stir the limp soul
of anyone fishing the marshlands off Savannah these
mornings, dreading the blowflies that carry pestilence
in their plump bodies, like Apache AH-64's fully armed.

WHAT IF IT NEVER STOPS RAINING

FOR HAROLD AND LIBBY

My friend Harold and his wife Libby are cruising
                    on a barge
on the Seine to Normandy, and I am thinking,
                    What if
it rains all the way to Normandy, and they miss
                    Monet's Giverny,

or the stamping grounds of Richard the Lionhearted?
                    Suppose
the Captain says on the intercom, *No landing today,*
                    and, uh, oh,
I am wondering what they will do in the barge all week
                    if they can never

escape the weather, if it turns on them like traitors?
                    What is it like
inside? Are there staterooms with all the amenities?
                    And if morning
awakens as night descended, what will they do?
                    I know

they are resourceful, but how can they enjoy reading
                    at those prices—
whatever they are—if they only see the landscape
                    through a porthole,
and someone knocks on their cabin door to ask them,
                    Que voudriez-vous boire?

then says, *Ce qui vous aimer avoir pour le dîner ce soir :*
                    pêchez ou le poulet ?
and that's it, served in their stateroom under wet towels.
                    They deserve
better—an adventure, escape into another history—
                    before they return

to serve the grace of mourning and its long memory.
                    So I check
the weather in central and northern France, hope it
                    will hold,
and they will return as is, but changed ever so slightly,
                    so no one will notice.

Part Three

AT THE LINCOLN DINER

Once I was sitting in the Lincoln Diner on West Main
                    with Dick Hetzler,
eating French fries doused in salt and thick ketchup,
                    while across from us,

on a stool, a large-boned woman, but not plump,
                    seemed happy
until we came in, or, rather, until Dick came in,
                    who, after downing

his fries and shake, looked at me, then at her,
                    and said loud enough,
She's not that fat, Ronnie! which spun her around
                    to give me

that special look reserved for barnyard clods,
                    her jaws
working overtime, a spot of mayonnaise gracing
                    her full upper lip,

as her boyfriend, a big dude, sat back, flexing
                    his forearms,
as if he would have liked to loosen my face but for
                    Dick's being there

to complicate his mission of defending her honor;
                    and Dick was laughing
so hard his eyes were wet with pleasure at my undoing,
                    so I said to him,

Why'd you go and say a stupid thing like that?
                    while I am thinking,
What could I possibly do to redeem myself to her,
                    without making

my good buddy the fall guy, the easy-going one who
                    lived on my street
and whose sister broke my heart five years later,
                    then married me.

A Blessing

for Jane on her 70th birthday

If my right hip aches when I first lie down,
I turn to face Jane, who always faces me
since her left side is a corridor of pain,
and as she drifts into a sedated sleep,

both of her hands twitch, as if a spirit
of unknown origin entered her frail body.
She holds my left wrist in her thin fingers,
as if to convince me of some belief, that

this is how it should be, or else she plays
in earnest with the fingers of my right hand,
so I cup her hand leisurely in mine, closing
it slowly, feeling her tremors until my hand

calms hers, and I whisper, *Time to sleep;*
and as she does, I count interludes between
breaths, longer than ever before but steady,
then release her, knowing how blessed I am.

Daisy, Daisy

I cannot shake the chorus of *Daisy Bell* beginning
                    "Daisy, Daisy"
from playing in my few neurotransmitters left,
                    maybe because
Daisy was the name of my father's mother,
                    who died
giving birth to a brother when my father was five,
                    which led
to his long circuit ride from one house to another,
                    until my father
was of legal age and which also led his father
                    to farm out
all his sons, turning my father into a quiet man,
                    a stutterer.
Or maybe the jaunty melody of "Daisy, Daisy"
                    and the ease
of its lyrics simulate the way I remember
                    the better years,
to recreate some of the decades between
                    my naivety
and my resolute drift toward death, as I recall
                    Billy Collins' poem
about a haunting song in his book *Nine Horses,*
                    a song worm
that writhed through his mind, as "Daisy Daisy"
                    does mine.

PLAYING GOLF

I was playing golf with my dead father on a course
     we did not know,
with borrowed clubs and golf balls that acted
      like out-of-round
marshmallows or ordinary puffballs when we
       tried to pick

them up, or else they surrounded our golf cart,
      as if to offer
themselves as free, but we finally found a tee
      where
two new balls sat up for us, as if on command,
      and we teed off.

My father hooked a long drive into a shallow pond
      but no,
into the first cut of rough where a pond once was,
      and I climbed
a steep bank and descended, without any pain,
      to find his ball,

which I did, or thought I did, but it broke in half,
      while my tee shot,
earlier, went as far I could hit, over a creek bed
      on a par four,
but it lay buried in a sand trap with a 90% angle,
      sand blowing

in our faces, covering our shoes and I was wearing
      work shoes,
when my father disappeared, left as he did once
      before,
almost 40 years ago, without saying goodbye, dying
      so quick

he only had time to tell my mother, *Julia, I feel sick,*
      then fell back;
and nothing was ever the same for her, or any of us,
      but mostly
for my mother, who slipped into a darkness from which
      she never recovered,

except in my dreams, where the two or three of us
     never argue
or complain, and I was so happy he wanted to play golf
     with me
that, when I found his ball, broken or not, I called to him,
     I found it!

SITTING AT THE END OF A LONG ROW OF CHAIRS

Sitting at the end of a long row of chairs
in a large hall, my father is wearing a gray
suit and vest, white shirt, and red bow tie.
His hair is still dark, with patches of gray,
and his legs are longer than I remember.
Before he steps up to the podium,
he is unsure of how to act, so he doesn't.
He crosses his legs, leans back slightly
in his wooden chair, looking straight
ahead, expressionless, as if he were
thinking about the design of a galaxy.

I am looking in from a side entrance.
When he sees me, he stands up without
changing his expression. He looks older
now. I am my age, older than he ever was.
He is much taller than I remember, so I look
up at him as if I were a child. In the hall,
everyone is excited that he has come, that
he will explain how to fix what went wrong.
He says to me, *This is a squirrelly place,*
a word I never heard him use before.
I say to him, *Yes, it is. But they love you here.*

South High Street

If it happens again, I am going to shut off
                    all corridors:
lock doors, board up windows, to keep out
                    whatever
continues to make that disturbing sound.
                    I ask myself,

who are they and why are they working
                    in the dark?
Is that a chainsaw I hear, or is it a grinder
                    or milling machine
and where? What are they up to at this hour,
                    as obvious as

EMS—lights flaring, deputies cordoning off
                    the scene:
a house (or is it a garage?). Wait. Hold on,
                    am I dreaming
once more? Will I sit up and say something
                    to the sound

surrounding me like a shroud, or haunt
                    the dark
like a ghoul and wake up Jane, as before?
                    Finally asleep,
her meds working, breathing quickly but deep,
                    her headache

boring into her old pillow, in the same bed
                    we came home to
on South High 50 years ago, where the homeless
                    found refuge
nightly in our basement but out before the sun.
                    Why should

we care, with three rooms, a bathroom, heat,
                    walking distance
to our work, groceries, whatever we needed
                    then—then—
all for us only, only a few glitches and mishaps
                    here and there,

like my scraping the side of my father's car
                    in our driveway
more suited for a bicycle, but, hey, we were
                    there together,
no car, no money, no promises yet unfilled.
                    Yes!

Waking Up Tired

Rising later now, I wake more tired than before,
                    when I used to walk
to the sky brightening and the frantic chirping
                    of birds, squirrels.

The lines on my face deepen, linger longer,
                    its T cells
worn down by too many passages, too many
                    revolutions,

while dreams once lost to time's generosity
                    follow me,
as when, in the wide living room of an airplane
                    that flew

in circles through narrow ways, I looked out
                    at our wing—
or was it our tail or nose—that barely missed
                    the green edge

of a building, and maybe that is why I wake tired:
                    too much
of the active life asleep, or too little, as I think
                    of you sleeping

on one side all night and part of the day, fingers
                    involuntarily
touching my back, as if to send me a message,
                    That it's OK,

your faint heart is beating and that, if you awake,
                    so will pain,
as it always does, one throb following another.
                    Should I count

your pain a blessing, as I do waking up tired late
                    in the morning,
with you still lying next to me, now stirring , still
                    holding on?

Night Calls

I woke to the ring of the telephone, which was
                                        not ringing,
then to Jane's soft, low voice calling, *Ron, Ron!*
                        as she slept,

so I sat right up, asking, *What's the matter?*
                        She never replied
but buried her head further into the pillow;
                        then I knew

at this early hour in the treacherous morning
                        what form
my dreams would take, if ever I fell asleep:
                        not the usual

frustration of not being able to find my room,
                        or my car,
or my way through absolute dark.   Oh no,
                        and I knew

if I slept I would awake to a day barely light,
                        to her pain
in hushed moans, to her life slipping away
                        from me,

no matter what I do or say or pray for silently
                        behind doors,
my head bowed, my fingers interlocked so tight
                        they bruise.

SOUTH ON THE INTERSTATE

I am driving down the Interstate at 85 mph,
                    trying to get
a specimen to the lab before it evaporates,
                    or does
something to invalidate its reading, and then,
                    well,
How do I explain to the doctor, or worse,
                    to Jane

what I failed to do when all the steps
                    are so
patently clear a child could follow them?
                    Meanwhile,
the interstate on this stretch is full of cops:
                    highway patrol,
sheriff's office, transportation police, and
                    what else

in unmarked cars, and what if I'm stopped?
                    Am I supposed
to say I'm trying to get a specimen to the lab
                    before it's too late,
that the medical world needs to know? O Christ,
                    keep my
arthritic hands on the wheel and my right foot
                    where

it's supposed to be. What's that behind me,
                    a Crown Vic,
from Vermont going south with a ski rack
                    or a cop?
So I'm nervous, but so what? What else can
                    I do
but *drive,* as Creeley wrote, *look out where
                    yr going.*

MY FATHER'S PAPERS

Last night I met my father in his prime before
                    I was born—
a late and only child—him a thin, tall boy,
                    full head
of hair that he never lost, and frowning,
                    as usual,

when he was displeased, which was often,
                    as when he saw
I discovered his papers without even looking
                    for them,
with arcane notes in his pure, clear hand—
                    as engineers

once had to have—and, puzzled, I wondered
                    how could
he have done these in his life before maturing,
                    at which time,
the same night, I also saw him as a man before
                    his death,

at ease, smiling, flashing his good, strong teeth
                    at everyone,
but not me, as if I were not there, and, of course,
                    I was not,
except in the tangled fibers of my dream mind,
                    though I had

his papers with me—in boxes, folders, loose
                    as manuscripts
threatening to fly away, as with the sad writer
                    in the movie
The World of Apu, whose only manuscript
                    of his novel

he tossed off the edge of a cliff, never to be
                    retrieved—
so I tried to get a cryptologist from India
                    to interpret
my father's prose and markings, but he was
                    indifferent

as to what lay before him, so I said to him,
                    in my best voice,
Here's a marked up newspaper from 1925.
                    What does it mean?
and I told him of my father's achievements,
                    as if I were

on CNN reporting the Pope's visit to a village
                    in Tanzania,
in the middle of the worst drought of the century,
                    which heightened
his indifference and that of his sullen wife.
                    The one item

I did not reveal to anyone was a note I found
                    in fragments
on ornamented notepaper without any lines
                    and signed,
Love, Alice, which I knew I could never disclose
                    to my mother,

so we all finally gave in to the blurring of time,
                    and I left,
my father aging more but still composed;
                    and, awake,
I walked to my den, looked at the package
                    of his writings

my mother wrapped in paper, twine, and plastic
                    in 1971—
when she wrote out the contents, precisely
                    as always,
in a blue, ballpoint ink—which I picked up then
                    and held.

A Clearing Over Caesars Head

When I have more than two glasses of Chardonnay,
                    I am different:
funnier, more friendly, more open, saying more
                    than I should
about what I would have kept to myself
                    a few years back,
and forgetting most of what I've said, until Jane
                    reminds me,

when she thinks she should, or if I ask her to,
                    and then I say,
Well, your memory isn't what it used to be, either,
                    what with
all the pain medication and other pills of all shapes
                    and colors
for her heart, which is closing up and her kidneys,
                    which are

shutting down, and she replies, *You forget, too;*
                    and we argue
for the first time in our union over who's right,
                    the basis
for arguments anywhere, and I remember the poet
                    William Stafford's
Right has a long and intricate name and the saying of it
                    is a lonely thing,

while our own words divide us into distant halves—
                    two memories
lost as in a gray smog over the Blue Ridge Mountains,
                    until the winds
shift for both of us, and, in the distance, a clearing over
                    Caesars Head,
where there is no right or wrong, just the trace for us
                    of a blue mist.

GROWING UP AMERICAN

I never spoke with my mother's father as a child.
      When I visited, he opened
a black purse, handing me coins, looking pleased
      that I had come. I never spoke

with my mother's mother, a large woman who
      gave me pastries.
He was slight, bald, wore a handlebar mustache,
      a tool and die maker with bent fingers.

Half a century and they never learned English,
      and my mother never taught
me how to talk with them, to know them apart
      from sight recognition.

She forbade me to say I was Hungarian, made me
      Anglicize their name,
deny their identity, as if I'd suffer for it, be called *Hunky,*
      or be taken for a Pole.

During the great migration, he came by himself, finding
      the harsh Maine coast
instead of Ellis Island, caught pneumonia, was given
      his Anglicized name, *Onion.*

In a small Hungarian town, his wife and first child,
      not my mother,
thought he died on the journey after not hearing from him
      in over a year.

The distance in English was incalculable, but that story
      ended happily,
and even my mother once forgave her heritage:
      in a Hungarian restaurant

in Würzburg, where she spoke Magyar with the server,
      as if it were only natural,
and it was. I listened and, selfishly, felt cheated,
      while she found herself.

When I first met my son's fiancée, a tall Muscovite,
      I asked her,
Do I look Hungarian? In perfect English, she replied,
      O Yes. You do.

Part Four

Passages

I am going to enter a room I do not know why
I am entering, maybe to pass through to a room
that may be smaller or larger than this one,
or that may not be a room but a closet, to find
a newer T-shirt to wear or to open a metal box
of my secrets. I am not dreaming, though
I might as well be, so I will retrace my steps
in this small house I call a cottage, to feel
better about my surroundings, to try to turn
on my synapses, to remember why I walked
down one short hallway to another, and then
stopped, because I do not know why and even
if I have never known, at least I thought I did.

Raising Me Up

In the sixth grade I learned I couldn't carry a tune
                    or even a note
when I sang *Zippity Doo Da* with Billy Vilardi
                    on the big stage

of our school, to parents, teachers, and other kids
                    at skit night,
without any props but a piano at Lincoln School,
                    60 years ago.

How I got paired with Billy Vilardi, later the Bop King
                    of our town,
is less a mystery than how I got there at all, except
                    I knew

the words to the song, and maybe I volunteered;
                    and so,
after years of humming tunes whenever I walked
                    or rode my bike,

and listening to my parents change the subject
                    whenever
I asked for piano lessons, and always made to stand
                    in the back row

by Mr. Humphries—the music man and piano teacher
                    of my first school,
All Saints Episcopal School, in another town—
                    my time came

on the big stage of Lincoln School; and, after singing
                    "wonderful day"
Billy's career began and mine, well, it didn't end,
                    because it lived

only in my head, and I am still amazed, stunned,
                    in awe
of the singular voice that, as Richard Powers writes
                    in a novel,

could make heads of state repent, while I fantasize
              I am blessed
for five minutes in church with the voice of a baritone
              like Josh Groban;

and, as the choir stands in preparation for its hymn
              during the offertory,
I rise, and, as the director raises her arm, I sing
              A cappella

Child of Blessing, Child of Promise and, when I finish,
              I sit down,
as if nothing out of the ordinary happened at all,
              and it didn't.

HAVING TO DO PENANCE

So the net was raised without our knowing.
                    Hey, that's
a given, to know or not know a coincidence,
                    while the leaves
perform their usual and, finally, boring show
                    of the season,
but perhaps only if you've seen enough leaves.
                    Meanwhile

the Germans work the fields until they die;
                    and, well,
our pioneers did too, before America discovered
                    infrastructure,
when Ben Franklin paved the streets, created
                    departments
of sanitation and fire, along with the first public
                    lending library.

In building a nation, Ben also tamed the French,
                    stroking
their women and being loved, long before we went
                    haywire—
as in the priest who forbade parishioners to take
                    communion
if they voted for a candidate in favor of abortion,
                    unless they did

big time penance—and maybe we should now ask
                    ourselves,
What do we really expect besides a mirror image
                    of our dreams,
the darkness we cherish, indeed love, support
                    vigorously,
until it becomes a chimera, like waves of heat
                    rising from roads?

Waiting for Malley

I was 19 and with Henry Grant, the only guy I knew
                    whose parents
could buy our college if they wanted to, in New York,
                    off 42nd Street,
waiting to meet Malley—a Brooklynite, smartest kid
                    in his class
and the one most unfitted to spend four years in Maine,
                    which he didn't,

which is another story—at a bar picked out by Henry,
                    who knew,
maybe, of the B-girls who worked it; and when we sat
                    on stools
facing the bar, two women older than us, but not
                    by much,
sat with us. A child in this stratum of interaction,
                    I listened intently

to the thin, pretty one talk of wanting to finish college
                    and support
her little boy at home. Meanwhile she and her friend
                    ordered
three bottles of champagne, for which no one paid;
                    When Ike
broke in on the black and white 12" RCA TV that sat
                    on top

of three rows of bottles—its screen began jumping,
                    as if
Ike were on a trampoline, while the bartender tried
                    to calm Ike down
by fooling with the vertical hold. Then the girls
                    retreated
to the bathroom, just before the bartender stuck
                    Henry and me

with a $48 tab, OK now but ball breaking in 1955.
                              Rich as he was,
Henry had little cash, and I had less, so we slipped out
                              of the bar,
made it to the indifferent street, met Malley, went
                              to the Garden,
and watched our team be hammered by Seton Hall.
                              As I boarded

the train at Penn Station for the two hour ride home,
                              I overreacted,
as usual, guilt like a tide rising in my soft head, until
                              I felt sorry
for the girl whose name I never knew with the little boy
                              at home,
waiting for his mother to cook dinner, put him to bed,
                              and begin studying.

Ice Storm

An ice storm in upstate South Carolina, and I am sitting
                    in my den
waiting for the power to cut off, when Jane and I
                    will put on
down jackets, lay blankets on the bed, climb in, hold
                    each other,
as the temperature in our cardboard house plummets
                    and we drift off

into hypothermia, to be found by our granddaughter Alex,
                    on a mercy mission,
who will cry out, *Nana, Papa!* to our gray, numb faces,
                    when I start
thinking of the one-ton rat that sloshed through
                    the swamps
of South America, four million years ago, and already
                    my dream

tomorrow in late morning begins to take shape,
                    not of a rat
with razor teeth the size of my fingers but of a dark
                    so deep
I cannot escape, as if in a black hole, yet I must
                    finger
my way out on a smooth, interminable wall—
                    or what seems

like a wall—to deliver a message I will never read
                    to someone
I do not know in a place I have never heard of
                    but exists;
and I think, again and again, in my own darkness,
                    of light and power,
while around me the universe holds on tight
                    like a lover.

THE MONTH OF THE YEAR

September—when schools start to get
                    serious;
deaths of the elderly begin their ghostly
                    climb,
pumping up statistics each year, while
                    sickness
goes to school, spreading its virulent menu;
                    new models

of cars pop out like hives in the classifieds.
                    Of course,
depending on where you live, you may be
                    dazzled
by the hues of the coming on of winter,
                    or on weekends,
by men and boys wrapped up and wearing
                    uniforms

hitting each other with impunity, as America
                    applauds.
You may close down your second (or third)
                    house—
or not—if your parachute was golden, like
                    leaves,
like real money, like the color of your life.
                    I am

a September child, born on the ninth,
                    a day
in our history on which no one important
                    was born
or on which nothing important happened,
                    and while
I do not contribute to the month, I am still
                    its child.

THE PICTURE

There is a picture in everyone's attic or bonus room
                   or loft in the garage
that you find when you are older, as if you were meant
                   to find it only then,
because before you would not know or care about it,
                   but on days like this

when nothing stirs, and you only want to take a nap,
                   you know
you should not give into your body's soggy rhythms,
                   like the patch
of wetland lying under the dark, wild maples in back,
                   filled with rainwater.

On this day, you should walk up the stairs, holding
                   onto the railing,
then sit in a ancient chair and remove the covering
                   of a dusty cloth or open
a scrapbook—and there it was for me: our living room
                   with ten adults

from St. Mark's Episcopal Church, the Rev. Kline,
                   and a woman playing
a portable organ, all heads sunk in dark hymnals,
                   maybe singing
my favorites then, *Holy, Holy, Holy* or *Fairest Lord Jesus,*
                   protestant favorites, too,

all except for my father, in a suit, like the other men,
                   his mouth shut,
thinking that his voice would rupture the sacred moment
                   of music, the rest singing
of the blessings or the torments or the love of Christ,
                   my father silent

but self-conscious, a quiet man allowing the church
                   to enter his living room,
when my parents only went to church on holy days,
                   but believed.
My mother must have scrubbed our house and baked
                   that morning, afternoon,

my father home from work at 5:20, eating, my mother
                    quickly cleaning up,
both of them dressing for that night: What was it for?
                    Why did they come?
In the roiling turmoil of my mind, wherever I am, I carry
                    this picture:

Our living room full of worshippers, or maybe just
                    the priest;
the rest of them candidates for a lapsed faith message,
                    on this night of song,
fellowship, and pastry—my mother's perfect gift—
                    an epiphany.

ENGLISH 101

On the first day of a class I never taught,
I asked the students if they ever played softball,
and when no one raised a hand, I told them we'll

play softball next class, and to prove how athletic
I was, I started to throw a ball that wasn't in my hand
and pulled up short, as if throwing nothing

through the air proved be too complicated, but then
a ball appeared, miraculously, a small ball,
like a golf ball but softer and looking like a baseball,

and, after I threw it, it crossed a body of water,
as on TV when Tiger Woods or someone else hits
a golf ball and it crosses the ocean, landing in Barcelona

or on a back street of Paris and a group of young boys
marvel at its bouncing on the cobblestones,
never coming to a rest, and while mine never went

that far it did glide over a creek like a Frisbee.
Someone in class said that didn't show him much,
so I tried to find a field to play softball at a school

I had never been to before, and even if I found the field,
how could we get there, play the game, and get back
to our next classes in time? Somehow I ended up

with a 10:48 appointment to see the dean, as the first
or last resort, and when I asked his receptionist, *How
long is my appointment?* she replied, *It's over at 11:00,*

which isn't much time to clear up the logistics,
or to ask where's a softball field and my classroom,
which I never found, but my ball just kept on gliding.

READING THE MAIL

As I was drinking my second glass of cheap chardonnay
              before supper,
I picked up a brochure from the mail, advertising items
              for those

who must have everything, when I saw a modified
              ping pong table
floating in the middle of a swimming pool with two guys
              trying to play

and, well, I thought, how silly, as I turned the pages
              to hammocks,
then to floats of equal value, and, once the second glass
              settled in,

I started, without cause, to think of Humvees without
              plating
to withstand roadside bombs and soldiers without
              Dragon Skin

under their combat fatigues; and, after pouring
              another glass,
I almost opened a thick envelope from the DNC that,
              on the outside,

asked, *Are you willing to put up with this White House?*
              but the one
I opened was from American Express, offering me again
              a titanium card

that cost as much for a year as a floating ping pong table
              or hammock
or float with a blonde dangling a long, tanned, sinewy leg
              off the side.

I took out the official letter, with a fake plastic card,
              embossed,
and read the pitch, until its print vanished like particles
              of sand.

FLIGHT

At first it was golf balls that looked and acted
                    like marshmallows;
then elevators that went everywhere but where
                    I wanted to go,
as in needing to get to the ninth floor on time
                    when it

stopped at the fifth, and then I could not find
                    anyone
to punch my ticket for the ninth. Once I saw Jane
                    riding down;
but when I tried to get on, the door would not open,
                    and she vanished

completely. The cage door of the next elevator
                    drew closed
in front of me, and I knew that I saw it before,
                    somewhere,
now appearing like the Phoenix of a thought;
                    Then I lost

my ticket at the departure gate for the plane
                    I never flew in,
as it taxied off the tarmac, stepped up into air.
                    Finally I woke up,
my body buzzing like an electric razor, my heart
                    not racing

but trying to run a mile in under six minutes—
                    at my age?
What is happening to me? Why? Wait, I think
                    it's all
about flight, so I reason this must be my wish:
                    to leave

the surface of my life, to rise above the earth.
                    Where
am I supposed to be going and why now in my
                    seventies?
Surely not into death, which is not in my equation.
                    Not yet.

THE POOL

In the pool the water is blue-green and tepid,
without end, though you can step out onto land
whenever you wish. The horizon is limitless,
but the water is in a pool, almost still, with slight
undulations, as if fanned by an invisible hand.

There is no night in the pool, and only you are
in the water, up to your shoulders no matter
your height, and the bottom feels as if you are
walking, not on the liner of a pool but on a surface
that is nameless, with a long, honored history.

Every step you take, your body steps out of itself
into another time, and pain is no longer a memory.
You are neither blessed by the waters of villages
in Europe nor by De Leon's lost fountains of youth.
This is the pool you have sought your whole life.

A BIRTHDAY POEM

When I die I am not coming back as anyone else,
                    or as an animal
even a predatory one, like a sleek jaguar or panther,
                    with little
to fear, or for that matter to love, or particularly,
                    as a tree,
to be precise, a Bradford Pear, with its one rush
                    of beauty,

and eleven months of gawky, angled limbs tossed
                    by irrelevant winds
and even rejected by a slick magazine because
                    of its fragility,
after being the darling of the horticultural gang,
                    the in-tree,
like a foo-foo girl to the media crowd on both coasts
                    and Miami,

so when mine died I cut it down and planted
                    Bermuda grass
after grinding the stump and removing the mulch,
                    a sad looking
lump in the middle of a lawn whose grass nearly died
                    from envy
of the precious tree. The new Bermuda looks like
                    the fresh grave of a child;

and I'm thinking what's really wrong with me,
                    now that
I no longer believe *Death is the mother of beauty*
                    but it's a knockout
of a metaphor that fooled me almost all my life,
                    the cradling
of our triad and the father of my deception:
                    RIP.

A Note on the Author

A Note on the Author

Ronald Moran was born in Philadelphia and moved to New Britain, Connecticut, when he was 10. He received his BA from Colby College and his MA and PhD from Louisiana State University. After having taught at the University of North Carolina for nine years, he joined the Clemson University faculty in 1975, and retired twice, first in 1998 and then in 2000. He served in a number of positions at Clemson, including Professor and Head of the Department of English, Associate Dean, and Interim Dean. In 1969-70, he was Fulbright Lecturer at the University of Würzburg in Germany. He has published ten books/chapbooks of poetry, including *Saying These Things*, the inaugural volume of poetry issued by the Clemson University Digital Press in 2004. Moran is the author of one book of literary criticism and co-author of another. His poems and essays are widely published in magazines such as *Commonweal*, *The Louisiana Review*, *Main Street Rag*, *North American Review*, *Northeast*, *Northwest Review*, *Pudding Magazine*, *South Carolina Review*, *Southern Review*, *Tar River Poetry*, and *Yankee*. Moran lives in Simpsonville, South Carolina.